God's Little Guidebooks

No.5 Love Mum and Dad

CHRISTIAN FOCUS

Sam and Katy have made a present for Dad. It is his birthday. He is very pleased when they give him a brightly coloured picture.

Mum and Dad are feeling tired today. Sam and Katy offer to help by tidying their room.

They try to keep quiet so that Mum and Dad can rest.

Dad has told Sam and Katy to be in bed by the time he comes home.

Dad is pleased when Sam and Katy have done what they were told.

Mum has hurt her arm. Sam and Katy offer to help in the garden.

They have fun sweeping up the leaves.

Sam and Katy are trying on some new clothes. They say thank you to Mum and Dad for buying them.

A friend of Mum’s has come to visit.

Sam and Katy do their best to be good.

Sam and Katy know that their Mum and Dad are very special.

God is pleased when children love and listen to their parents.

Sam and Katy remember God's fifth command.

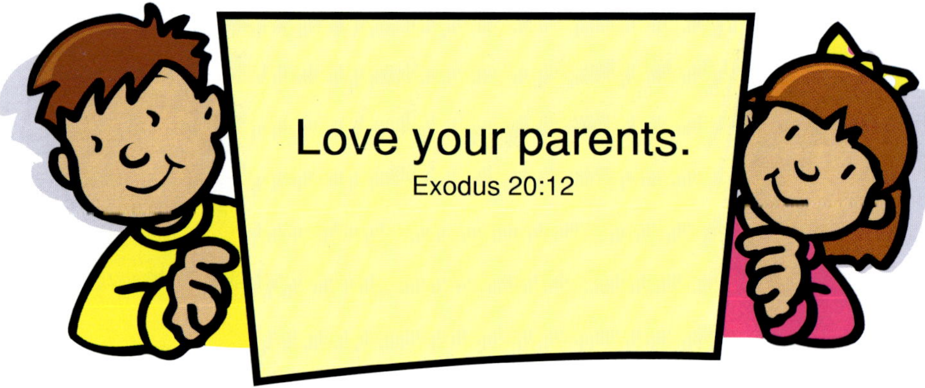